The Book of Skeletons

poems by Rachel Vigier

PEDLAR PRESS | TORONTO

ACKNOWLEDGEMENTS

The publisher wishes to thank the Canada Council for the Arts and the Ontario Arts Council for their generous support of our publishing program.

LIBRARY AND ARCHIVES CANADA
CATALOGUING IN PUBLICATION

Vigier, Rachel

The book of skeletons / Rachel Vigier.

Poems.

ISBN 1-897141-05-X

I. Title.

PS8593.I35B65 2006 C811'.6 C2006-902725-0

First Edition

EDITED FOR THE PRESS Molly Peacock
COVER ART Michael Pittman
END PAPER ART Emma Koosis
DESIGN Zab Design & Typography, Winnipeg

Printed in Canada

The Canada Council for the Arts since 1957 | Le Conseil des Arts du Canada depuis 1957

ONTARIO ARTS COUNCIL
CONSEIL DES ARTS DE L'ONTARIO

we human beings need each other,
and in that there is already directness

SØREN KIERKEGAARD

Contents

Blue receding

They do this every day.
He watches her blue coat recede
until he loses her to the morning rush of the Exchange.
How big is the marketplace? How big is the city?
And where does she go when she rounds that corner?

One child was found with a ball in his hand.

You know (*don't you?*) how the mind does this
rushing inside the skull until it hesitates
first against a movement barely glimpsed
then a phrase barely heard
holds them close
closer still.
But why?

Why
hold a child
pushed
in a trench
against
a blue coat
losing itself
in a crowd?

Aubade

I snapped the stranger's mask into place
then we climbed, single file
with the others, from the shelter to the street.
Inside, someone had been praising her Lord
shaking with disbelief.
It was impossible to stay in the building.
Outside, the air kept coming down
flecks of light
falling with the air
to the street drained of colour.
I was walking without thinking *why* or *where*,
had suddenly become with the others a great herd
circling away from burnt grassland
puffs of ash and dust rising from our feet.
We were travelling in the same direction
listening with the body but I wouldn't let myself think
how we had been that morning, a man and a woman
reaching out of sleep, bodies turning into each other
how I had pressed my ear flat against your cheek
the roughness of it, eager for your breath
already strong, as we found our way
waking to a good morning.

SANCTUARY

He touched my arm.
You need help he said quietly.
I'm fine I heard myself say
but there, again, the touch, on my arm, light
like a bird brushing past.
You're bleeding. Please come in.
At least let me wash away the blood.
A church had opened its doors.
I leaned into him, only a little, but enough
for him to catch a slight turning,
first in my foot and then into him, a stranger
leading me up the steps
through the open door, the dark inside.

To think endlessly

To think endlessly, the way one dies—
—MAURICE BLANCHOT, *The Writing of the Disaster*

In the ambulance, the light shines clear through
the tubing. Outside
something inhuman is spreading. Here
we are trying to breathe. A rattling stretcher
pushing against the speed
of going.
Who is dying?
Are we getting
close to the hospital? The paramedic sits
hands hanging
blunt between his knees. Yesterday
he nursed a beer with his twin, saw
how their hands almost *connected*, swears he remembers
touching *in utero*.
Their mother has already called, trying to reach them both.
For now no one answers
or tries to help, the light
shines steadily, suddenly
the rattling stops and someone
speaks in grunts commanding an instinct to surface. Where
were we (*was I*) going
when they shook, took us?

Shoes

He washed my feet on the emergency ramp
at the hospital and I—
strapped to a chair
not knowing when I'd need to run next—
could only bark *My shoes! Give me my shoes!*
as hands
cut off my shirt and others
sprayed ash from my body.
He looked at me
like Mary Magdalene must have looked
at the stranger that time,
kneeling and weeping, lifting her hair.
He handed me
first one shoe, then the other
and I held the dusty pair, tight, to my chest
as he held my feet
over a pail, but gently, so I wouldn't feel
the cut of the rim against my skin
only his hands, dipping and pouring
water, his face shining up.

Natural History

after Elizabeth Bishop's "In the Waiting Room"

This is a waiting room
in a hospital in New York City.
The room is full of bent heads
and loose hands. No one
is speaking and no one
is reading *National Geographic*.
A nurse leads a patient in
and settles her into a chair.
I haven't been thinking
how the body
will remake itself
until I turn my head,
a slow swivel
into the eyes of the man
sitting next to me.
Something is forming
in his face and I see now
how I am this patient
and how in the next days
his arms will shake and shake
from holding snapshots
up to strangers as he checks
and rechecks
all the posted lists of names
until every list
is blank.

There are creatures who live
at the very bottom of the ocean,
with parts grown so large, the organ
dwarfs the body in its drive
for survival. In this deep sea,
fanged teeth grow larger than the mouth,
intestines transmute to pure hunger
taking over a whole body,
and where there is little light
luminous innards and enlarged eyes
search the dark and pressurized cold.

I turn from his eyes
to the door where I see
my mother collapse
against the frame, her hand
clapped to her mouth.
I stand and wobble
toward her reaching, a child
on her first legs, while outside
in New York City:
light and ash and warmth.

Apparition

Later I see it from the air, the crowd
streaming over the bridge, turned away
from its city, stuttering and choked with dread.
On the street at the foot of the bridge
I accept a stranger's hand to join
these ordinary spectres, ashen-faced,
come to the end of a violent day when
looking up I see him—the poet of Brooklyn!—
appear among us, spanning the bridge
swinging from cable to cable, shouting
and loving the shadowy crowd below—
I see you my orderly citizens! I see you face to face.
I see you practising our art in full splendour!
I am with you, you men and women, you keepers of this civic dream!

Dying for beginners

Surprised by the mind—*with* the body—in pain

its tightness knotted in the flesh

like the ligature of a hangman's knot

cutting through the windpipe. The end

is sudden and complete and it doesn't matter

where the breath goes. What matters

is absence—sudden—felt

the sound of our family breathing in the same bed

the weight of our children resting on my chest

the big rustling of the pin oak on our street.

Paradise

In the chapel the undertaker flips a switch. From below
the whir of a machine kicking in, and the floor opens
to a casket rising, then settling, with a click, into place.
On the flight over I remembered our conversations—
dance, New York, friends—and how it had started
in the studio. Just us *in* the body. With you
moving us into its laws of motion, how the body
gives in to gravity but only up to a point
of suspension when torso arms legs
lift catch and swoop the loop of energy
in every muscle—the fall and recovery in every movement.
We believed the body could tell everything
(but we'd always said what we meant, too). And now,
leaning into your body, to your face
so softly closed, I mean to say one more thing
as I slip a snapshot of the city you loved into your hands.
The body—*ours*—is paradise. I heard you say this once.

Notes toward the other

It was only a short distance, perhaps forty feet
of walking to a dim light through a mesh
of particled strangeness. *Am I dead?* but not said
so clearly. More a vague feeling of the body
working to lift the chest without knowing
what would come next or what exactly had come before.
When I saw him stepping in the ruins, his foot lifted
searching for a clear place,
I didn't know what I was looking for. I put my hands out
and walked toward him but did not think to call out—
my body still had its own use for the breath,
measuring possibility
in each shallow movement of its chest. Now I understand
I was searching for an *us*, and look how sure
my body stepped in this reaching—not for the hand of a god
painted against a cracked blue dome—but for a shirt,
yellow and soft, the back of a stranger.

On this day I want to ask

Do you believe in ghosts
    riding up and down elevators?

Is your imagination intact
    or is it worn out from praying?

Do you jump at loud noises?

Do you ever see yourself
    holding on to wrecked beams in broad daylight
    weeping until you can't see anymore?

Is there someone you now know you love?

What will you feel later
    when you open a faucet to wash your face
    and clean water
    pours into your palm?

Will you wonder if small acts
    like the flutter of butterfly wings
    really can start a hurricane?

Will you wonder if every question has an answer
    or what happens to a question
    if there is no answer?

Do you still jump at loud noises?

And will you ask yourself, now and every night
    in transparent dreams
    why?

Magical thinking

1 In a motel room a young man shaves his chest at dawn
doesn't see
how the hair clumps and sticks to the rusted sink
as he rubs the skin
then tosses the towel, torn and thin.

In my city
I rise with the light edging in
the feel of hair thick in my hands.

2 The dust will not settle.

Every day at 4:00 AM crews water the streets
to damp down the dust. Every morning I kneel
to scratch the sidewalks thick with remains
and store the dust in a box at the office.

Up and down the street I find others
like me, mad magicians in suits,
collecting remains to make talismans
as if these objects can save us.

An empty box engraved with the word *dust*.
The torn picture of a daughter's wedding.
A broken record labelled *destiny*. Black pearls.
The word *blue* written three times.

In the Ossuary: St. Catherine's Monastery, Sinai

The desert light is clear on skulls
stacked neatly in a cell—the smell
of thyme in the doorway
gives way to mold in the ossuary.
The monk is young and fierce.
In the ossuary, he explains
how we are all the same
when after a year, each monk's corpse
comes out of the ground,
rotting and rotten
skull pelvis scapula
thoracic cage femur ulna
all disarticulated sorted and stacked
in separate cells except for St. Stephanos
sitting on a stool alone in a glass case.
He's a full skeleton, draped in gold-trimmed
black velvet robe, velvet slippers
and velvet cap perched on his skull.

Dry pitted hard: I walk from cell to cell
thinking this is the way the dead are
until I see one hand reaching
from a stack of arm bones, green-grey
velvet skin still covering its bones,
dried ligaments binding its phalanges.
I flex my own fingers
against a palm dried by desert air
as St. Stephanos looks on and the young monk
urges us away. One day, this hand, too,
will fall in a heap and the young monk
will sweep and gather

each bone in his habit
perhaps remembering whose hand this is
lighting a candle in the chapel
swinging a censer against its chain
collected, finally, in prayer
against a dark and dusty robe.

The bath

The head turns in my palm and my body tenses
guarding against
denting the skull on the sink's hard edge.
It doesn't feel like a skull, really.
Skull is hard boney tough but this infant skull
malleable cartilaginous like the body of a jellyfish
would take the impress of fingerprints
from the faintest press and the fontanelle,
pulsing at the top, would burst like a fleshy peach
from the lightest indent of a thumb.
Seven years later, she's in the bath and this time
I'm washing her hair, listening as she tells
of Lincoln's assassination. Of course,
she holds her own head and it's a real skull now,
sutures fused, fontanelles closed.
She's precise in the telling: how Booth waited
for the act with the loudest laughter,
the great jaw shaking open with each guffaw
before the shot entered the skull
right there, she points to her own temporal bone
circling the knob twice before drawing a line
into the cranial vault to the exit
through her frontal bone. Lincoln died the next morning
and Booth broke his leg jumping to the stage,
she finishes, as I rub her head harder
to erase the dotted lines of death
she's traced there. My body hasn't forgotten
its instinct to guard though I know it's not enough
against this history, and her coming of age.

The book of skeletons

By Jesuit standards
she has reached the age of reason.
Tonight she means to teach me skeletons,
the art of seeing
through flesh, drawing bones
spongy articulated full-blown
motion. Here's a team of skeletons
kicking a soccer ball. This one
lunges to her first goal. That one
is furious. See the puffs of dust
as she stomps away, phalanges clacking.
Here's a skeleton
vaulted in a pirouette and another
flying on a skateboard, perfect figure eights in air
daring to believe these bones
whose bright marrow twists
coils spirals and springs.

Santa Trinità Bridge, Florence

Built in 1567, the bridge was bombed by the Nazis in
1944 to slow the advance of the Allied Army.

The sandstone feels gritty and warm to my palm.
On the buttress three boys laugh, suddenly pop open a can.
I lean into the ledge watching my daughter run
from statue to statue, the four seasons,
each marking a corner of the bridge. She stops
before *Inverno*, *Autunno* craning her neck
looking for *Primavera* who lost her head in the war.
She doesn't know we've lost her father and her sister
in the maze of streets beyond the bridge
or that I'm thinking of rebuilding
and how much I've wanted to cross this bridge
rescued from its rubble, sandstone and marble
hauled from the river
piece by piece put in place
by masons aligning and fitting
with ancient chisels and mallets a kind of truth
I've wanted for years now, feel joined now in these stones.
At the other end of the bridge, my daughter calls:
she's found *Primavera*. I cross the bridge
to tell her how *Primavera*'s head remained lost
for twenty years buried in the river's silt
until one day the current lifted and rolled it to the bank
like an offering from the river to spring
and to citizens, each day, crossing the bridge.

Tango in the Zurich Platzë

¡Mi corazón! What odd pairings!
Children chase pigeons in the plaza
as the accordion stutters then wails. A dreamy girl
leans into a dumpy man, while a woman curls
a thick-veined leg around a man in dreads
and a Mohawk-haired kid, hips swivelling,
drags his partner lightly across the floor.

These people are not beautiful—they are ravishing.
Torsos proper and straight, joined
just barely at a hip, broad suntanned arms
splayed across bare backs.
How correct this civilized display
of sex in the *Platzë* on a Sunday afternoon
when all the shops are closed
and all the churches open.

Look, here's a woman tangled with her partner,
quick light steps dazzling big sure feet,
her flesh giving way
to the pull of knowing what she knows
until…*Mama*…a child cries out and she hops
clip clop clip down three stone steps
to a girl—all knobbly knees and coltish legs—
wobbling on skates. With the tango still on her face,
the mother steadies her child, then arm-in-arm
the two slide away, not once looking back
to the dancers still dancing.

Birthday Poem

1 We left the baby with my parents to go wading knee-deep
in snowdrifts piled in the churchyard across the street.
Under my coat my chest hurt as the cold slid in
sharp singular pinpricks. Afterwards I lay for days, sick and chilled,
wrapped with our baby in bed. The sky matte and grey
snow coming down clouding the spire.
I got used to our breathing, the flannel smell and newborn skin.

2 *We're old Not even married*
the woman in the bed next to mine
giggled over the head of her newborn.
Looking deep into folds of skin
from over my own infant's head we laughed
roaring like gods who'd just played a trick
on this mortal mortal world
until suddenly
we turned away, struck dumb
by what we'd just done.

3 Into the silence
of the maternity ward in the middle of the night:
My roommate's gone
with her son and his father, the protective slump
of shoulders, blankets and thick coats,
the backs of new parents filling a doorway.
Goodbye, and good luck! A new reality.
What time is it? A squeak of shoes passes in the hallway.
Voices lift and fade. The silence of a room
where a curtain lifts and falls. How something happens

between rise and fall: ruffled shapes, gravity and currents,
a rattling window, cold filling the room.
I can't bring the baby in until the room warms up the nurse scolds.
Soft officious thump, the window closing. The curtain pulled back and still.
Look how bare the trees in the park across the street.
The granite boulders forced up.

FOOLISH HISTORY

Now I know I am a diver,
I have been lowered into the depths
of foolish history
—EDVARD KOCBEK, "Moonlight"

You jump to the window
shouting at a flash in thc sky
as I scramble through the room
invoking your grandmother's ghost,
the young mother, boiling water
against soldiers in Bucharest.
To throw in their faces
when they come through the door.
And now, we are in it too
not lowered into the depths
but *in it* as we stand
naked to the window
tensed for the next blast.
When it comes
we can't even laugh or feel foolish.
Thunder. It's just thunder.
We fall into each other as the rain comes,
knowing we are in it
boiling water against enemies
making weapons
from pens and bedside gadgets
with our girls asleep in the next room.

Flight

1 Humans on the run from each other.
We were afraid it might end this way
so I researched old maps
from creek's end upstream to the channel downstream.
All up and down the canal, I found others doing the same
inspecting underbrush and following old trails, until one day
we tried it—floating away in a silly canoe we found
moored to an abandoned dock, expecting the current to carry us out.

2 We walk the girls to school and inspect the rotting canal,
a creek once widened by acts of Congress
to make way for barges and ships.
Now, jellyfish bob in brackish water and crabs
stick to thick-planked sides or, cracked and dry,
litter the flat tops of pylons.
At low tide, the silt on the bottom gives up its garbage:
crowbar, bicycle frame, fire hydrant, hubcaps.
It's what you never forget, a dumping ground
of deep secrets an old neighbour assures us.
Over there, cars pushed off the edge
bodies forced in too (that unsaid).
Paint chips and oil slicks float by.
Underneath, minnows and brown shadows drift and disappear.
We want to believe something lives. Yesterday a kid
casting his rod for mackerel and bass
showed us his catch, lifting a line of fish
twisting and twitching
from the shiny bottom
of his pail.

3 Later, we talk by the window watching a couple
stroll over the canal. We're trying to remember
where we've been—our lives spliced together—
when suddenly she jumps in
after hitting her companion with a cane.
We'd meant to tell each other more
but the rescue interrupted our train of thought.
The helicopter, circling in
descending by our kitchen, blades thudding,
the thud in our bodies
scaring the birds, circling the canal,
silent and panicked, concentrated in their appeal
as a rescue worker, holding on to very little,
swings out the open door and in a one-armed swoop
fishes her out, a prize catch, dangling
for a moment, mid-air. Was it then
we made our choice to go on
looking out of (*into?*) paradise?

The slant of evil

In a back room
flooded with light—
the house in Amherst
stilled by her might

the poetess in white
would speak of it
weirdly—wrestling
with her Self.

On the murder of the poet's mother

For Paul Celan

Every night the poet
hears the shot
feels for it

in the nape
of his own neck
thinking of

every permutation
of death
in a death camp

crossing border
after border
the distance

never enough
the language
always an echo

Explosion

In the first moments it's just laws of energy, the body lifted
and flung like a strip of sheeting torn from scaffolding
or a tree ripped by its roots toppled by an instance of force
greater than mass, but later what stays in the body
surfaces as what's endured
in the half-light of every grey dawn
when slivers of fear appear
in a familiar room before anyone rises or stirs
and where, even on ordinary days, I have to make myself
notice the warmth of a body deep in sleep
the stillness of a house and street.

Somewhere

Her children are sleeping in the next room.
Overnight the air has changed, deepening the sound
of small bodies turning over in sleep.
She remembers the barrel of the gun in the doorway
the shock seizing her face, the unvoiced
not like this then *too far from home.*
In the hall, at dinner, she'd heard the announcement—
curfew, patrols, children in bunkers at all times.
The children she'd taught that morning, giggling,
mimicking her accent as she'd tried their mother tongue.
Hurrying to her room that night, she'd seen a face in the dark
coal black eyes blinking in a halo of light, a mother
rushing to the bunker with her child's medicine.
She'd stopped then, to breathe the desert air
listening—somewhere—inside the ground—children
playing, and laughing, at what grown-ups do.

Here

A public school in New York City, 2001.

Every day this child can’t wait.
He runs to the block corner
builds a tower
demands everyone
leave the building
watches his father
take the steps
two-at-a-time
hurls himself
arms wide
like wings
into the tower
blocks scattering.

The other children run away run away run away.

This is what we did:
We kept talking
the languages we knew best.
We made our signs
in big block capitals.

We told the children not to worry.
We told each other to *make* life normal.

Sometimes away from the children
at night or in rooms shut tight
we told ourselves other things.

Are we like them? Or not?
Would we kill them too?

We ask the children to be better than us.

Shevone raises her hand.
Ibrahim writes a poem.
Sarah plays a trick.
Bibi crosses her fingers.

Class trip, Lower Manhattan

Africa. Europe. Asia. America.
The kids sit cross-legged in front of the museum
sketching the monuments of the continents
as the Wall Street crowd makes its way, crossing the place
where Peter Minuit bought the island from the Lenapes—
sixty Dutch guilders' worth of cloth, kettles, axes, hoes,
Jew's harps and *diverse other ware*. Exactly twenty-four dollars.
What kind of history is this? And how wrong it all seems.
On the way in with the kids, through the tunnel from Brooklyn
I count exit lights as tires slap the tunnel pavement.
How far to the end? How far to the end?
It's true that one day, death came too close
brought by strangers with strange beliefs
but they're dead now and I'm not so what more is there to tell?
The children are done sketching, run to the fountain in the park
as the teacher walks to a fence, lecturing:
In 1776, this is where the Patriots,
fresh from reading the Declaration, marched with a crowd
to topple the statue of King George the Third.
They smashed the crown, cut off his head and melted his face,
his iron arms and legs, to make Patriot bullets to kill Loyalist troops.
Feel the nubbins on the fence where they knocked off crown finials.
As I trail behind, fingering broken tips, Alex and Elias
run circles by the fountain and the two Sarahs swap lunches.

Visiting St. Michel, Venice

We've come to where Venice buries her dead.
We're alone on this island and it's drizzling
as we walk through the cemetery gate. The girls go ahead,
I stop by the family vaults reading the names
chiselled above the lintels. Through a grille door
a vault with marble pieces, dried flowers
and broken vases scattered across the floor.
Next to it another, impeccably kept, two straight-backed wooden chairs
set side by side. Imagine the comfort of it,
the coolness of the vault, the hours
of talk fading, and then, the growing silence of it
seeping deeper and deeper into the walls.
From behind a wall I hear the girls wailing.
They've reached the children's cemetery.
I go around and see them near small mounds
reading names and counting dates,
their bodies, still and straight.
As they stand between cypresses, three in a row
growing by each grave,
I notice how the girls are as tall as the trees
and think how to come here each year, you might notice
the growth of the trees
measured against the length of a grave
that only sinks deeper and deeper
into the precious soil of this island.

Follow the City

1 March 3, 2002

How the organ swells as the tourists swing their hair
and the locals stand in reverence. Obedience.
Look how the woman in blue angles her body to the altar
away from a woman in red staring at the priest reading St. Luke.
Cast out a demon that is mute. Every kingdom divided from itself becomes a desert.
The bell tolls the quarter hour. The arches multiply against each other
vaulting over the brass eagle perched on its globe.
A hooded lady, though late, knows exactly where to pick up the sermon.
My mother was a heretic her voice confides *Pick yourself up*
The wafer cracks over the microphone.
Who will stand and choose themselves?
A bald-headed man walks down the aisle, hands clasped,
a starchy god crumbling in his mouth.
In the half-empty church, another
searches for a pew as if there were a seat, just right, for each of us.
The organ turns ominous. A black cassock
disappears through the archway. Quavering. Wavering.
We all face god and disappear.
The whispering behind me picks up again
as if we have the power to help ourselves

2 In the subway

I can't. I can't. I just want to wait. Deep in the tunnel
a train rumbles and approaches
catches the cry of the child yanking his mother's arm
then rushes by
ruffling papers strung on a newsstand. The platform sighs
steps away from the edge
as a transit worker scuttles behind scraping a dustpan
against the tiles. Here's someone just doing his job
where everyone walks, then stops, a complete stride.
A couple lean against the dirty wall counting chips of blue
in the mosaic, two ships steaming to port.
(Down here transportation's the theme.)
She twists his tie while somewhere on the F line
into Brooklyn, a lady bundled in blue
leans her forehead into a pole trying to place her body
in this metal surround. She watches her feet
take tiny steps, feels how this body bobs and accepts
the bounce of the train, its twists and turns,
how smoothly the walls in the tunnel slide darkly by,
while between her hands
the grime of the pole, the dirty light and
used-up looks slide into her skin.

3 Saturday on the grounds

The sun is finally warm where it matters.
On the grounds the old man on the bench
doesn't blink or move his head. Next to him
a woman talks
to no one in particular as she eats her cake
straight out of the box:
It's all that's left of him, a flag folded in a frame
sitting on his dad's desk. Somewhere
there's an urn, empty except
for a handful of dust they brought in a baggie.
She stops to sip her drink
and tug at her pajama bottoms. I close my eyes
listening to the rope slap against the flagpole
and when I look up she's gone, the empty box
tossed to the ground.

4 THE BLUE OF THE SKY

"The blue of the sky" is what best expresses the sky's emptiness...
—MAURICE BLANCHOT, *The Writing of the Disaster*

On the big slat bench
a dapper man sits cross-legged, facing
the blue of the sky.
There is some thinking in his face.
He swipes his mustache, unfolds his legs, folds his hands.
Out of boredom pigeons approach.
Kids selling candy, not successfully. He gets up
walks down the street to the graveyard and sees
a band of 3-year-olds running through graves.
(They feel the dead can't harm, don't they?)
They've invented a game
Yellow hood   Blue jacket   Pink sweater
Yellow hood   Blue jacket   Pink sweater
flashing between stones.
Below him the subway rumbles sending its vibration
through the dead
sandwiched between the living and the living.

5 Follow the City

Can you imagine the breath of a general
heaving a country into being?
Minuit walked on this spot. Sometime later,
Washington too passed through.
What does space keep of any body?
Minuit didn't sit on this bench,
though over there he once kicked through the fort's front gate.
As for Washington marching through
tipping his tricorne hat
he's now captured in a stately pose, on the Street
towering over millions, a free market
fruit of his economy.

From the other side of the wall
this was wilderness. Now concrete towers,
trees on rooftops, red insects
crawling a white field of shirts, suntanned arms
locked in defiance, helicopters and dragonflies
hovering over water.   Holy.   Holy.   Holy.
After all this time the City reeks
but everyone still comes
to water for cool.

I want to stop and arrange things:
the stitching on the baseball
reflected in a stone relief,
children walking across the river,
the politics of the moment,
a pink hat flying into water.

6 Guilty?

A lunchtime crowd trickles to the steps of Federal Hall
while across the street a man in a tan coat stops to pat the bomb dog.
Why shepherds? Can he do anything else? The dog,
ears perked, sniffs, stands at the alert and sits down. All the tourists,
zoom lens extended or pocket cameras held high, look for the best shot.
The street worker sweeps butts into his dustpan
drags away the bin as the Hercules unit points down their guns.
A woman in a blue coat waves her hand, signs for lilies
from the guards at the Exchange. A man with a limp thumps his briefcase
against his leg. The keeper locks the dog in a cage and walks away
as someone stands on George Washington's pedestal.
For a moment he's declaiming Washington's address to the troops
then becomes another tour guide stealing attention
from the stranger across the street preaching Revelation
my name my word shuttedth and shuttedth. Everyone walks
or sits or stands. It's the law. The sound of pipes falling
echoes. Metal on metal clanging down the canyon
against the syncopated roll of a corrugated gate rising from the back of a truck.
What happens if you shift your gaze to a small hole? The doubting Thomas
of Wall Street rises but it's OK to proceed slowly, person by person.
Here's a tourist with a cigar in his mouth, waving and coughing.
Here's an orange-and-blue striped shopping bag strolling by.
Here's a boy running round a pole as Mom and Dad study a map.
(Everyone's always trying to orient themselves but it's a proven fact
the map's distortions are real. Just try to place yourself somewhere.)
And here's a man posing sadly for himself. Flash. Oh look he wants another. Flash.
The sun keeps shining and you keep asking what's here at this corner?
Until the body tells you to push off. There's daylight elsewhere.

Who wants to tease out layers? Let's just keep stacking and stacking,
building and tearing down, building and tearing down
where George Washington keeps watch until today
when someone somewhere in a cell well hidden finally confesses
first to himself then to country *I didn't mean any of this.*

7 Dear Old Marshall at Dine-Around-Downtown Food Fair, Lower Manhattan

We do everything we can to escape the present.
—MARSHALL MCLUHAN

The ribs! Get the ribs! All the best are here from the oldest to the boldest.
She can barely walk. It's barely spring, certainly not summer. The roast beef
smells burnt. The crab cakes are too small but stacked, high and just so.
The woman in blue dabs her chin with a crumpled napkin, throws it
to the shadow of a bird flitting across the plaza. She's done
and gone now—disappeared—as the bald man licks gravy from his lips.
In her place three men squash hamburger buns, a signature dish. Press and scoop
ketchup from the sides, spread the napkin and wonder briefly
who's looking and taking notes. Bird shadows keep coming. A red tie strides by.
Cheesecake. Don't! Don't! Try the gorgeous cupcakes.
This is food. A brown paper bag sweating oil. Hand to mouth. Hand to mouth.
The cooks look harassed. Pull another tray from the stack
as the ever-present broom and dustpan drag by. A piston releases
from the buzz of construction and TV cameras whiz thru
to capture the *renewal of*. It's true, it's sunnier now and there's more light but...
the vase of Calla lilies tips into chi-chi white mousse cups
setting off a clue from dear old Marshall: Find a headline
and ask someone here, now, in the sun, eating on the ground
where the granite cracked, about the dead
made dead by mistake. No wonder the birds are anxious.
There's a lot of stooped shoulders and most of us are too fat.

8 Vertigo, May 20, 2002

Do I pray (or say) looking out the window: Tall's as tall as tall can get?
What happens when you move up, one floor at a time, for sixty-two counts?
From here you see the cloud cover drop and in the East River
a tug tow a barge, slowly out of view. Look how the mind
matches the grey of the clouds to the grey of the river
thinks *gun-metal-steel* then pockets of trees, stacks of ochre,
brown, dirty limestone, off in the distance a copper roof.
Last week a hawk flew so close its wings might have brushed the window.
Without thinking I stepped to the glass raising my arms to give it shadow.
What if Icarus had these wings? Or what if angels
with great wingbeats crashed through saying everything
except *Forgive me?* Mostly, it's blimps, helicopter fly-bys, planes
that may or may not hurt but that's not what I want to say.
What I want to say here is a simple story:

My friend and I are afraid of heights but one day, not so long ago, we went
to the top of the tallest building in our city. We almost couldn't step out
along the terrace. Fortified. Walled. It seemed nothing could ever come down.
We looked down and out. Over the blue of the sky to the antenna on its twin.
A stranger (was it a lady in blue?) took a picture of us.

How to Speak

1 A few days after September 11, 2001 my husband took a picture of me with our younger daughter. We were sitting on the play table in the dining room. My head was tilted back. My eyes were closed as my daughter brushed my hair with a hairbrush too big for her small hands. Whenever I look at this picture I can feel how carefully she worked around the injuries on my face.

On September 11, my husband left early for work. I left our younger daughter at home with our sitter and dropped off our older daughter at school on my way to work in Lower Manhattan. A block from the subway I heard a woman call out to someone on a stoop. I heard the edges of talk as I walked by.

Planes. Accident. No.

I got off at the Wall Street stop and walked up the stairs to the street. There were too many people on the street. I remember asking myself: Why are papers floating in the air? And why can I actually *see* the air?

A crowd had gathered around a red car at the corner of William and Wall. The doors and windows were open, the radio announcer saying something I couldn't understand. I asked two women what was going on and I heard the same words, this time not on the edges of talk.

Planes. Accident. No.

I had been keeping a notebook in my bag in which I'd been writing poems for a book about my sister's disappearance. I was afraid of the words I'd been writing about her life and her disappearance. I didn't know it then but I was going to become even more afraid. Afraid of separation and silence, what I used to call death. And then afraid of words, again.

I know the exact place I was standing when I knew I would die. I was running east, running and then trying to get up from the force and the shock of the South Tower collapsing. For a moment, alone and in the incongruous blackness of a bright sunny morning, I didn't just think I would die. I knew I would die.

There is a difference between thinking and knowing. If I know something I can locate the idea in space, in a particular body, on a particular street, in a particular place.

Every day I pass by the exact place I was standing when I knew I would die. Sometimes I stop to stand there—but never for too long.

2 A year and a half later, the green market is back across the street from its old home beneath the Trade Center. The men are back, shuffling backgammon pieces on makeshift tables. The food carts are beginning to come back. Office workers are starting to congregate in the park the way they used to.

There's not much left of the park. The trees are gone, shattered by the force of the buildings collapsing. Now, the park is all stone slabs and steps. Still, the green market is back.

I watch the people for a moment. At one booth a man is selling fresh-picked Jersey strawberries. The berries are warm from the sun. "It's good to have you back," I say to the vendor. He smiles. "Thank you. It's good to be back." I buy the berries in a simple exchange of words and hands, shifting goods for money. It's what we used to do.

On September 11, 2001 as I was running from the collapsing building I threw off my backpack. Along with my poetry notebook I lost poetry books I was reading, Wallace Stevens and Keats. All things considered, it wasn't much to lose.

Six months after the attack, when my family and I come back from vacation the letter from the New York Police Department property clerk is waiting for me at home. They have found some of my lost property. I hope it's my notebook. My husband comes with me to Police Plaza where an officer directs us past a lineup to a door. Through the door, in a hallway, we see a man sitting on a sofa. As another officer takes my papers, she directs us to sit next to him.

"Are you here..." the question trails off and then picks up again "...for yourself or someone else?" he asks. I understand immediately what he means but I can't yet bring myself to say I've survived.

"And you?" I reply.

"My sister," he says simply.

As he tells us how he lost his sister who worked on the 94th floor of the North Tower he keeps repeating *It's too hard to talk about It's too hard to talk about* but he keeps speaking, his voice breaking, as he tells us how, from his workplace across the street, he saw the plane hit the building she was in.

"Right then I knew. It's too hard to talk about. I wish they'd stop calling me. Ten days after, they called. They found remains. Then they called a few months ago. Her credit card. And now this. Even though I knew, I kept going to the Armory. The worst was the day there were no more Jane Does on the list. I had to go back home to tell my sisters and my mother, 'There are no more Jane Does.' I've gotten used to the open space now..."

what remains without remains

All the strangers in this hallway begin to cry. No one can speak.

3 Lately, my children and I have been watching a cartoon called *Courage the Cowardly Dog*. We are all attached to Courage, though I'm not sure why. He's an ugly pink dog who never speaks clearly. Mostly Courage yelps fear and surprise, and more often than not his heart pops out of his chest beating extravagantly before him.

Last night, after watching another episode of *Courage the Cowardly Dog*, I found my seven-year-old sobbing in her pillow. She couldn't answer me when I asked what the matter was, so I sat and held her, waiting for her to speak. Finally, she squeezed out a few words. She was gulping, her mouth working itself open and closed, as she struggled to control her breath long enough to say, "I think I can tell you now." And then she had to stop again as her breath overpowered her words. "I can't," she cried, waving her hand and turning into her pillow.

It was a clear moment of what it takes to make words and of how the body relies on this instinct of making words to relieve or transform feelings, ideas, experience.

4 Today is the first day I've been able to sit on the terrace and listen to city sounds early on a Sunday afternoon. We live in an old brownstone in Brooklyn. Our neighbour and his wife raised their children in the house next door and in their backyard there's a tall forty-year-old tree that casts its shade over three yards. When we first moved in, they told us how they had gotten the tree from a friend's wedding they'd attended when they themselves were newlyweds, a potted tree they'd rescued from the wedding decorations to plant in their own backyard. A breeze ruffles the leaves. I hear a few birds chirping now and then, the trickle of water from the fountain in the backyard. No drought this year. Is this the quiet that's wanted all over the world?

5 ...the red of the car at the corner

...the voice of the announcer carrying the sound of disaster

...the voice of a stranger urgently repeating, "This woman needs help. This woman needs help."

...the realization that I am this woman

...the dry feel of a hand on my shoulder

...the look of astonishment on my daughter's face, "Mommy, why are you coming home from work looking like that?"

6 I am well aware of how fortunate I am. Within hours of the attack I was being treated at one of the best hospitals in the world; I had a home with running water to go to; within days my children were in school again as usual. Yet the fact of the attack remains and I keep asking myself the same question. *What does poetry have to do with this?*

Some days it feels like too much to ask; other days it feels like not enough. Lately it doesn't feel like the right question at all. But what is the right question? What question is there to reconcile the act of making poetry with the death, confusion and fear that came with the attack? And with the sudden and sharp clarity, too, that permeated everything?

In the days after the attack, New York was encouraged to go about its business. And we did. So I began to write again because this is my "business," because it's what I've always done to think through what I don't know or understand. I still want a poem for all of us who got on the subway after the attack and went to work next to sixteen acres of remains that burned for months. "How's the air today?" we'd ask each other before going out for lunch.

7 One day at work I listen in to conversations on the elevator: "My daughter's soccer coach was killed." "My sister's brother-in-law died." "We've been to three funerals already."

One day my husband and I go to eat at a newly opened local restaurant with beautiful woodwork. The sign at the door asks us to leave a contribution for the families of the carpenters, all of them now dead, who had built the restaurant. On the morning of September 11, they'd been working a job in the Trade Center.

One day I look out my office window and see what I think are trees lining the ramp into the site. It is a dark rainy day and I puzzle over the trees until I realize what I'm looking at. The firefighters in their black slickers have lined the ramp as they carry one of their own out of the remains.

One day not long after the attack we stop in at a restaurant close to our old home in Manhattan. The proprietor comes to our table and, looking at my bruised face, asks in a very tactful way if my husband has hurt me.

When I say I'd been injured during the attack, he tells us about his friend who had been artist-in-residence at the Trade Center. "When I got the call that he was dead, I said that's not possible. He's never up that early in the morning." On the night of September 10, he'd been preparing for a show and slept over at his studio.

One day, eighteen months after the attack, my five-year-old sits in my lap to ask what happened to me when the buildings fell down. "Did you cry?" she asks. "Who helped you? Were you afraid? Did it hurt? What did they do to you at the hospital? I'm glad you didn't die. How did you get home?"

These are the moments when the question of poetry seems thin and out of place. These are the moments when the question of poetry is most necessary.

8 On the subway this morning the woman across from me was reading a religious newspaper. I was reading a book about poetry after Auschwitz. We looked up sharply as the train stopped in the tunnel under the river. The panic in her face matched mine. There has been talk of fresh attacks. The train started up again and we returned to our reading, each trying to understand in her own way what is happening in our time.

Later, I sit on the steps of Federal Hall where the Declaration of Independence was first read to Patriot troops in New York and where George Washington took the oath in 1789 as the first president of the United States. I'm looking at the scene in front of me now, wondering how to speak about the helmeted, heavily-armed, flak-jacketed police officers who have been standing here since September 11, 2001; the pickup trucks loaded with sandbags that have been blocking the streets since then; the checkpoints with the bomb-sniffing dogs; the crowd of office workers and tourists walking through this maze of security and fear, looking and not looking, as the saxophone musician on the corner plays *Somewhere Over the Rainbow* one more time.

In her introduction to *The Best American Poetry 1990*, Jorie Graham writes that "the poet must move to encounter an other, not more versions of the self. An other: God, nature, a beloved, an Idea, Abstract form, Language itself as a field, Chance, Death, Consciousness, what exists in the silence. Something not invented by the writer. Something the writer risks being defeated—or silenced—by."

The silence immediately after the collapse was shocking and palpable. Others who were there have also remarked on this eerie silence that followed the roar of each building collapsing on itself. What exists in this silence? For a moment, there is only a woman invented by History, Chance and Death, bleeding and walking in shock, away from the disaster, with her arms stretched out in front of her, moving toward what seems to be a patch of light in the dark not knowing if she is buried alive in a pocket of rubble or outdoors still, until she reaches an other stepping carefully through the rubble and then an other bent over in difficult breathing.

9 *Writing is evidently without importance, it is not important to write. It is from this point that the relation to writing is decided.*

—May, 2003

NOTES

Epigraph: From *Søren Kierkegaard's Journals and Papers.*

APPARITION

The phrases "*I see you face to face*" and "*I am with you, you men and women*" are from Walt Whitman in "Crossing Brooklyn Ferry."

MAGICAL THINKING

Early news reports about the attacks on September 11, 2001 indicated that letters to the suspected hijackers instructed them to shave their body hair before carrying out their mission.

HOW TO SPEAK

The title "How to speak" is from a quote by Eavan Boland in *Object Lessons* (W.W. Norton & Company, 1995). "How to speak. I believe that if a woman poet survives, if she sets out on that distance and arrives at the other end, then she has an obligation to tell as much as she knows of the ghosts within her, for they make up, in essence, her story as well. And that is what I intend to do now."

In sections 2 and 9 the passages in italics are quoted from Maurice Blanchot, *The Writing of the Disaster* (University of Nebraska Press, 1995).

ACKNOWLEDGEMENTS

ON THIS DAY I WANT TO ASK was commissioned by CBC Radio for special programming commemorating the first anniversary of the 9/11 attacks.

An earlier version of GUILTY? appeared in *nthposition* online.

SHOES and SANTA TRINITÀ BRIDGE, FLORENCE originally appeared in the *Literary Review of Canada*.

Thank you to Beth Follett, Molly Peacock and Zab for your vision and belief in my work and thank you to my family and friends for your love and help.

ABOUT THE AUTHOR

Rachel Vigier is the author of a poetry collection *On Every Stone* and a book of non-fiction, *Gestures of Genius: Women, Dance, and the Body*. Her work has appeared in journals in Canada and the US, on CBC Radio and in an anthology *September 11, 2001: American Writers Respond*. She was raised on a farm in Manitoba and now lives with her family in New York City.

GALILEA NIN